CHICAGO

CHICAGO

Gary Irving
&
Stephen G. Parker

SKYLINE
PRESS

This book is for the friends at Radio Station WCFL,
who share the Good News in Chicago, and for my wife
Janine, my friends Karl Fliehler and Sandi
Forrest–Oberreich, and my brother Tim, for providing
me with company on my many trips around the city.

GARY IRVING

Produced by Boulton Publishing Services, Inc., Toronto
Designed by Fortunato Aglialoro
© 1986 Chicago Review Press
SKYLINE PRESS is an imprint of
Chicago Review Press

ISBN 1-55652-047-6,
Printed in Hong Kong
by
Lammar Offset Printing Ltd.

*E*arly morning in Chicago. Up from the lake the sun drifts, rising bright and grandly soaring higher, pricked by the masts of yachts moored in the harbor. A summer breeze ruffles the slowly swelling surface of the water, shattering the glassy plain into myriad bits of glitter, soundlessly, as if the passing of the light itself had stirred the calm.

The sun continues higher and reaching past the shore illuminates that 'magnificent mile' of facades. The sunlight is warm, the shadows cool this time of day, and the avenues are filled with light, and breezes that flap the unzipped jackets of pedestrians and mess their hair, but no one cares. The sun continues up and up and gliding past its zenith leans the buildings' shade across the streets.

Along the lake the parks billow with the bright green leaves of elm and oak and the windswept sky is high and domed deep blue, mottled with midwestern cumuli, harbingers of evening thunderstorms. The solitary, white, grey-bottomed clouds pass overhead incessantly and shadows glide up the marble, steel, and glass exteriors, slide down the other sides to skim over streets and parks and darken for a moment the breeze-whipped waves.

In Grant Park the Buckingham Fountain sends up hissing jets of water arching high into the air. The falling mist sparkles as it drifts out over the border of lawn, over the railing and into the iridescent faces of children who stand there laughing, calling, as the coolness wets their skin, soft voices in a gentle rain of light.

Chicago is an inspiring subject for the photographer because its architecture, flora, fauna and people offer all the great themes of photography. Chicago holds a unique blend of these elements. Even when considered one by one they set Chicago apart from other metropolitan centers.

Chicago's role in the development of modern and contemporary architecture is undisputed; it was here that Louis Sullivan designed and erected some of the first skyscrapers, and that Frank Lloyd Wright did much of his work. But perhaps the most dramatic architectural development in Chicago was introduced by Ludwig Mies van der Rohe.

Van der Rohe arrived in the US from Germany in 1938 and that same year became Director of the School of Architecture at Chicago's Armour Institute, later the Illinois Institute of Technology. Van der Rohe brought to Chicago, and to architecture, an approach to urban design which unfurled glassy veils from the sky, broad sweeps of reflective surfaces demarcated by slender ribbons of steel in a variety of finishes. This international school of design created an effect antithetical to that of the old Chicago architecture. Now, instead of massiveness and a sense of unbearable weight, of an earthbound formality often endowed with grotesque decoration, there were constructed visual illusions of airy weightlessness; windows to the sky. This buoyancy was further emphasized by designing the first floors of many of these buildings to be inset from the outer edge, creating the impression that these structures were not supported from below, but merely anchored there to prevent them from drifting away.

Chicago architecture has not been the same since. Indeed, Van der Rohe's concepts have been refined to the point where the steel mullions themselves have been done away with, so that in many instances only a single expanse of uninterrupted glass is presented, flat or curved, sometimes at angles to the sky and to the street below. The opportunities for photographic interpretation are limitless. At times the deeply tinted, sharply mirrorlike quality seems the ultimate in statements regarding what is and what appears to be; gazing up at one of these contemporary structures one sees not the building but instead a wall of glass in which is reflected the buildings opposite, an illusion within an illusion. The camera multiples the illusion once again. Images of doubled images. It is an architecture both utilitarian and imaginative, an architecture created for the real need of human beings for light and openness, but an architecture which also toys with human logic, not flippantly, but with an elegant sense of humor.

To appreciate the role which nature plays in Chicago, Daniel Burnham's *Plan of Chicago* must be considered. Published in 1909, it was the blueprint responsible for much of Chicago's future development. Burnham had been the guiding force behind the World's Columbian Exposition which opened in May of 1893. Situated in Jackson Park (of which only the lagoons and what is now the Museum of Science and Industry remain), the fair was the testing ground for Burnham's ideal city; a place with people in mind, their need for space and physical beauty, entertainment and sport, factors helpful in countering the recognized inevitable stresses of city life. This was the philosophy behind Burnham's *Plan of Chicago*, a plan calling for broad avenues radiating out many miles from a central axis to ease the problem of transportation in and around the city. The central axis itself was to be the lakefront, specifically a large harbor just off a grand civic center. The lake tied in perfectly with Burnham's designs. Earlier he had envisioned development of the lakefront from Grant Park south to Jackson Park. But the *Plan of Chicago* called for the conservation of nearly twenty miles of shoreline parks.

Urbs in horto, 'City in a Garden', is Chicago's motto, and it is one of the few really large cities that have not cut themselves loose from the earth. Much of this has to do with the lake, the perfect backdrop for any city, and Chicago's prime source of relaxation and recreation. But it also has to do with the city's park system, considered one of the largest in any metropolitan area, with more than 65,000 acres of forest preserve meandering along its western boundaries, and with miles of boulevards running through the city. Some of these boulevards have been allowed to decay, but driving along them it is not difficult to see what they were and what they could be again.

Nature is always close at hand, and it is the resulting juxtaposition of nature and architecture that comprises so much of Chicago—Chicago against the backdrop of the lake and parks, or vice versa. Both views exist. For the photographer, a panorama of possibilities.

*W*inter on the lake. Above, the sky gleams a pristine arctic blue, stripped clean by the cold, hard Canadian winds. Seen from the lakefront north of the city the skyline pushes out darkly from the shore, the pale winter sun beyond etching the buildings' edges in its silver light. Along the walks and beaches the naked trees stand in rows, their upstretched, outspread limbs and branches knitting delicate patterns of black lace into the azure sky, patterns trembling in the wind. The wind gusts down among the trees and sweeps up clouds of ice crystals high into the air. They prism the sunlight into momentary circles of faint colors, diaphanous traces of purple, red, yellow, and green.

The beaches and jetties lie covered with strange, unearthly shapes, created where the waves and frigid air have glazed with ice the boulders piled along the shore. When the wind is from the east ice clogs the water, a dangerous maze of jagged ridges stretching out for several hundred yards or so. There the high waves explode onto the ice, shooting up white geysers, and from the shore one can hear the rhythmic murmur of these watery collisions. The ice-packs grind and creak together, undulating gently as the waves slide under them. But when the wind is from the west it often pushes the ice out into the lake, leaving the water near the shorelines dark and clear. If the wind then dies, ghostly forms rise, vapor condensing in the cold air, streamers of mist lazing up into the sunlight through which the skyline seems an illusion, dim vision of another world.

*B*ut for all its architecture and its parks, Chicago is most of all people. Even in winter the lakefront is not deserted. Chicago has its share of diehards and winter-sports enthusiasts. Walkers and joggers take advantage of the walks and paths; among the trees and out on the snow-covered playing fields and open areas cross-country skiers glide smoothly—or, depending on their expertise not so smoothly—along.

Comes spring and the ice and snow dissolve away and the grass and trees begin to green, the days growing warmer as the sun moves higher in its path. Out on the lake the spring winds lash the water and after a thunderstorm monstrous waves rock the shoreline in spectacular fury. The first good rain washes the city clean after a winter of dirty snow and salt-stained cars, leaving it sparkling in the light. The parks become more populated as those Chicagoans not hardy enough to have ventured out during the winter now emerge. Then one day it's warm enough for the beach. No one knows when this day will occur each spring, but when it does, EVERYBODY heads for the lakefront. Homes and apartments are deserted, offices empty, and just about every kid in school plays hookey. If there ever was an unofficial holiday, this is it.

On good weekends all summer long the beaches and lakefront parks resemble nothing so much as one huge block party. Volleyballs and frisbees soar through the air, bicyclists and Sunday strollers crowd the walks, while those intent on developing their tans methodically turn themselves, slathered in oils and lotions. In the park-pavilions and on the benches old and young alike play chess with a passion oblivious to the kids wheeling by on all-terrain bikes, thundering boom-boxes lashed to their handlebars. Chicagoans are fanatical about clear, warm days because Chicago weather is as unpredictable as Chicago politics. A day in the seventies may be followed by several in the fifties and with rain, so you catch the sun when you can.

Chicago knows how to have a good time, and not just at the beach. The city's other favorite pastime is going to a ballgame. Boasting two major-league baseball teams, the Cubs and the White Sox, Chicago's roster also includes the Bears (football), the Bulls (basketball), the Black Hawks (hockey), and the Chicago Sting (soccer). But there are many activities for the amateur as well, the most popular being softball. There are an estimated 3400 softball teams in the city alone, with another 2600 teams in the surrounding suburbs. These include 16-inch, and slow and fast-pitch 12-inch.

Sports aside (heaven forbid) there is still plenty to do in Chicago.

During the summer there are more than enough art and ethnic festivals to keep one busy. The most well-known of these is the Old Town Art Fair, set up in Old Town just north of the loop where the streets are narrow, most of the brownstones wonderfully restored, and where the trees bend lazily overhead. Several hundred professional and amateur artists set up their works on the sidewalks in an area several blocks square. The streets are blocked off to automobile traffic and the crowds wander freely about, inspecting and admiring the artwork. On seasonal days the residents leave their front doors and windows open to the breezes and sitting on their porches or in their front yards, watch the people go by. The street becomes an extension of the living room, an effect as delightful as the artwork on display.

Then there are the many art galleries and museums—the Art Institute, the Shedd Aquarium, the Adler Planetarium, the Field Museum of Natural History, the Museum of Science and Industry. Chicago has its share of theaters too; the Blackstone, the Shubert, the Goodman, the Steppenwolf, and many others, including several improvisational theaters, Second City being the best known. Chicago is also a city of music. There is, of course, the renowned Chicago Symphony Orchestra and the Lyric Opera but Chicago is best known as birthplace of the blues, home of jazz. Each summer blues and jazz festivals are held in Grant Park, always well attended. But what to do after the show? Chicago includes an almost unimaginable variety of restaurants, eateries, and clubs, the result of the city's vast array of ethnic groups, that range from the Old European which made up the city originally—Irish, Italians, Jews, Germans, Poles—to the third world, the more recent arrivals—Orientals, Hispanics, and East Indians.

There is no end of things to do in Chicago, things to learn and see, places to enjoy oneself. Chicago was made for people. But to capture the meaning of this city on film calls for a return to the lake. Chicagoans are proud of many things, but most of all that, with the kind of pride one has for a symbol that represents the city's past and present but which is also useful and beautiful in its own right as well.

Without the lake Chicago would probably never have been established, since the city was originally a trading post, dependent on the lake as a waterway for trappers and traders. The lake still serves that purpose, although now for the shipping industries. So in that respect the lake represents what Chicago is at heart, a town of working men and women. And today the lake is also the primary source of relaxation and recreation. Having a good time has always been a priority among Chicagoans. Yet on a higher plane there is the visual beauty of the lake and its interaction with the sunlight, the weather, and the skyline. Chicago is a place to work and play, but more importantly, a place where one can contemplate natural beauty and the fruit of the human imagination.

*I*t is an early autumn evening and the sun, lingering in the west, has spread its last light out to the city, an orange hue that gleams upon the western sides of the buildings, tinging them the color of gold leaf. Here and there the sunlight glances down the length of a street into the faces of commuters hurrying to catch the trains home, their shadows lengthening behind them. On the el platforms and in the train stations people stand, reading or just waiting, the last of the day's light falling obliquely on faces and hands. The sun slips lower and the light disappears from the streets, touching now only the upper stories of the skyscrapers and in Lincoln Park just skimming the tops of the trees. Drivers flick on their headlights and Lake Shore Drive becomes a pulsing river of light, ebbing and flowing along the lakefront.

Out on the lake the day's breezes have stilled and the water is calm, surging gently like someone breathing in sleep. Far out a lone sailboat motors towards the harbor, its sail lowered. Street lights flicker on and in the buildings lights begin to appear, dim at first, brightening as the twilight deepens. Then it is night and soon a full moon floats up, casting its shimmering light over the slow swell of the harbor. Out on the lake an excursion boat mutters along, easing through the calm, a wave flecked with moonlight curling away from the bow. Leaning on the railing, the night breeze cool on your face, you look towards the city's skyline, staggered geometric planes of twinkling incandescence, green and red, blue and gold, mirrored in the lake, that vast reflecting pool that gives back the same unfathomable and marvelous light.

STEPHEN G. PARKER

1 A field trip on the North Side; the hot days of summer find thousands of children in groups of all sizes exploring the parks, libraries, museums and zoos.

2 Trees along Jackson Boulevard in Grant Park fade away into February's fogs.

3 (*right*) A small boat floats in the copper-colored sunlight against the silhouettes of some of the tallest buildings in the world.

4 Members of the band relax before the long parade down
Dearborn Street, on Poland Constitution Day.

5 (*right*) Flying a kite in Grant Park.

6 (*left*) A watchful lifeguard on the 57th Street Beach seen against the backdrop of a brilliant summer sky.

7 Modelled on a fountain at the Palace of Versailles in France, the Buckingham Memorial Fountain is one of the largest in the world—and is also one of the most frequently visited spots in Chicago. It has a central stream with 133 jets of water, some of them spouting up 200 feet in the air.

8 (*left*) The arch salvaged from Adler and Sullivan's demolished Stock Exchange Building is now located outside the Goodman Theater and frames this view of the city to the north.

9 A game of chess by the lake on a fine afternoon in June.

10 (*left*) Reflecting off the Sears Tower, the westering sun gleams back at the Eisenhower Expressway.

11 Strolling on the promontory at the North Avenue Beach.

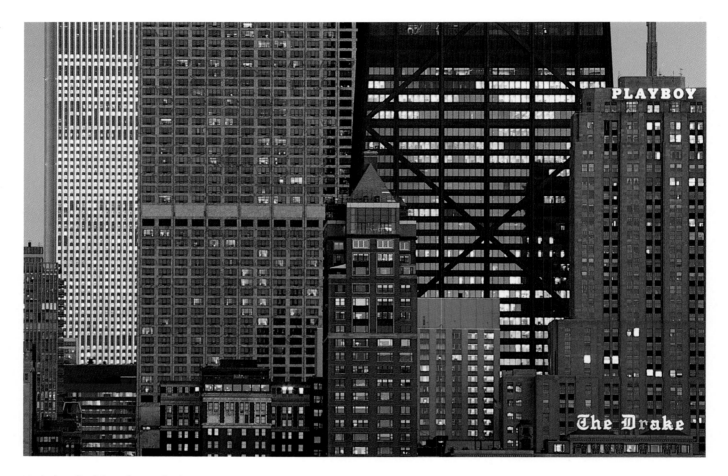

12 A detail of facades at dusk.

13 (*right*) A study in superlatives—the view from the
Observatory of the John Hancock Center. The Sears
Tower on the right is the tallest building in the world. The
Standard Oil Building on the left is the fourth tallest in the
world. The Hancock Center itself is the fifth tallest in the
world and the largest to combine both·commercial and
residential use.

14 A sculling crew having an early morning workout on Lincoln Park's
south lagoon.

15 Anglers try their luck near the Adler Planetarium.

16 Sunrise on North Avenue Beach.

17 (*right*) Sailing on Lake Michigan in the cool of the day.

18 The Art Institute of Chicago, one of the outstanding museums of the world.

19 One of Chicago's best-loved traditions is simply that of summery
afternoons on the beach.

20 Underneath the elevated tracks downtown.

21 (*right*) Frenzied trading in the Chicago Board of Trade building, largest grain exchange in the world.

22 Oldest of Chicago's Polish churches, St Stanislaus Kostka (1881) was home to the world's largest Polish parish in the late nineteenth century. It is a masterpiece of Italian Renaissance style, appreciated for its architecture and its art.

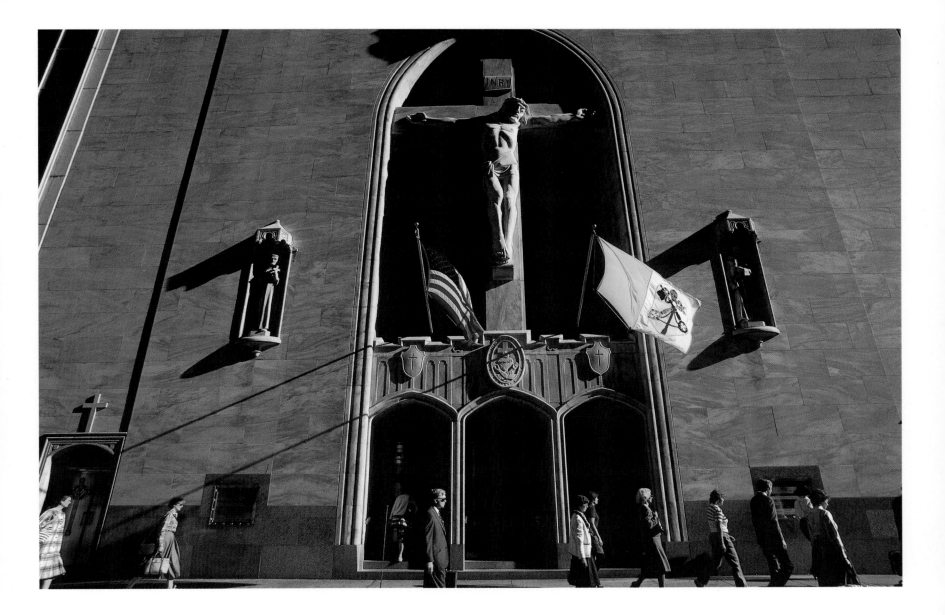

23 This massive crucifixion by Arvid Strauss dominates the facade of
St Peter's Church on West Madison Street.

24 On Sunday mornings an open-air market gathers on Maxwell Street and in the adjacent area near South Halsted Street. The market offers everything from used clothing to antiques, from garden produce to plumbing fixtures. The tradition of holding a market here goes back a hundred years.

25 The Chicago Board of Trade Building in
the Art Deco style stands at the end of the
La Salle street financial district.

26 Gold Coast townhouses—only minutes away from the Oak Street Beach and the 'Magnificent Mile'.

27 (*right*) A pool on the grounds of the Art Institute reflects early morning light on the facades of Michigan Avenue.

28 This steel sculpture by Picasso was given to the city by the artist himself. Mysterious—and controversial—it dominates the Richard J. Daley Plaza and has become one of Chicago's notable landmarks.

29 (*right*) Outside the massive McCormick Place Convention Hall, on the Outer Drive.

30 (*left*) Winter joggers on Cannon Drive in Lincoln Park.

31 Winter sunrise, Lakeshore Drive.

32 Main Lobby, Railway Exchange Building.

33 The bronze doors of C. D. Peacock's
venerable jewelry store.

34 Two exhibitors in the 57th Street Art Fair, the oldest outdoor art fair in the midwest, held each year on the first weekend in June.

35 (*right*) A garage sale complete with cycle-rickshaw rides during the 'Sheffield Garden Walks' held every July near the campus of De Paul University.

36 The main stairway of Burnham & Root's Rookery Building was
designed by Frank Lloyd Wright, and is one of the many architectural
landmarks that make Chicago a city-scale museum of the art.

37 'Fighting African bull elephants'—an exhibit in the Stanley Field Hall of
the Field Museum of Natural History.

38 (*left*) Fishermen on the North Avenue promontory; Chicago's skyline in the background.

39 The Lincoln Park Zoo; flamingos sheltered from the chill of a February morning.

40 In spring and summer cold, dry air from Canada often collides with warm, moist air from the Gulf. The afternoon sky darkens and a tornado threatens; but the condition can be very brief—only an hour after this photograph was taken the sun was beaming down again on the Kennedy Expressway.

41 (*right*) Steam rises off the lake on a frigid January day.

42 (*left*) Summer fun includes a ride on the paddle-boats at the South Pond
in Lincoln Park, near the Zoo.

43 Afternoon on the 'Magnificent Mile' along Michigan Avenue.

44 Jam-session with a drum, syncopated by the roar of a passing speed-boat.

45 A lone angler waits with patience as morning comes back to the city.

46 (*left*) Winter moon on the lakefront north of Belmont Harbor.

47 Skaters on the North Side enjoy the last of the afternoon.

48 (*left*) From May to September the Buckingham Memorial Fountain is floodlit at night with a display of constantly changing colors.

49 Dress rehearsal of *Cinderella* on the stage of the Auditorium Theater. This lavish production has become a popular tradition, and is performed by the Chicago City Ballet, the city's first major classical ballet company.

50 (*left*) The Chicago St Patrick's Day Parade is such a mammoth event that even the river is dyed green for the day. Hundreds of thousands turn out for the grand parade. Here some of the people taking part await their turn to join the procession down Dearborn Street.

51 Wrigley Field, known as 'the friendly confines' on the North Side, is the home of the Chicago Cubs.

52 (*left*) Sixteen-inch softball is an exclusively Chicago tradition, played nowhere else. There are thought to be about 6,000 teams of twelve-, fourteen- and sixteen-inch softball in the Metropolitan Chicago area.

53 Comiskey Park on the South Side is the oldest park in the major leagues and is home to the Chicago White Sox.

54 951 Chicago Avenue, in Oak Park, home of Frank Lloyd Wright, was built in 1889 when Wright was 22 years old. When the house was renovated in 1895 part of the expansion included this barrel-vaulted playroom on the second storey.

55 The sounds of the masters in a summer evening float out above the skyline from the Petrillo Bandshell.

56 and 57 Chinatown at the junction of
Wentworth and Cermak, a great place to
eat and shop.

58 (*left*) Boarding an excursion boat on a summer evening in Chicago harbor.

59 The La Salle Financial District; the Continental Illinois National Bank and Trust Building at South La Salle Street and Jackson Boulevard.

60 Jumping rope at a picnic in Lincoln Park.

61 Columns of the Civic Opera Building.

62 (*left*) Testing the water at Fullerton Avenue Beach.

63 Annual Sandcastle competition at North Avenue Beach.

64 Late afternoon at the Buckingham Memorial Fountain.

65 All kinds of good things are to be found at the Maxwell Street market, but best of all is the sound of the blues that has made Chicago its home.

66 A meal at the Berghoff is another of Chicago's fine traditions.

67 (*right*) This sculpture on the Michigan Avenue Bridge commemorated the Fort Dearborn Massacre during the war of 1812. Subsequently a new fort was built at what is now the junction of Michigan Avenue and Wacker Drive.

68 The 'Sounding Sculpture' of Harry Bertoia in the reflecting pool of the
Standard Oil Plaza.

69 Some of the 10,000 runners that take part in the Chicago marathon, a
26-mile run through the streets, parks and neighborhoods of Chicago.

70 Balloons brighten an overcast day and lift the spirits at the start of the marathon.

71 (*right*) The Museum of Science and Industry draws four million visitors a year to 14 acres of exhibits that include such remarkable displays as a full-scale coal mine and a World War II submarine.

72 The shoreline seen from North Avenue Beach.

73 Seen here through frost-patterned windows, the Old Water Tower is lit up for Christmas, a traditional feature of the season for the festive crowds of shoppers on Michigan Avenue.

74 (*left*) The Fourth Presbyterian Church, across from the John Hancock Building on Michigan Avenue, has a quiet courtyard that offers a little haven on one of the world's busiest thoroughfares.

75 A new day is softly reflected by the top of the Art Deco tower on the Board of Trade Building. The mass of the Sears Tower rises to fill the background.

76 Sailboats moored near the Shedd Aquarium at dawn.
The aquarium houses some 10,000 species of fish and
marine life.
77 (*right*) The Railway Exchange Building reflects the
morning light from its eastern facade.

78 The shoreline of Lake Michigan seen from the observatory of the John Hancock Building. For a different vista from the same point of vantage see plate 13 and the lights of downtown.

79 This view on Michigan Avenue embraces several of the finest examples
of the Chicago style, topped-off here by the clocktower of the Wrigley
Building, completed in 1921.

80 A quiet note on which to end—the skyline softly reflected in the lake.